Reactions to Dave Morrison's Poems:

"Dave Morrison is wide awake and paying attention. This latest collection is a testament to his ability to transform ordinary scenes into potent, lively poetry. "fail" is loaded with poems that are honest, exuberant, and at times laugh-out-loud funny."
Sudasi Clement, Poetry Editor, Santa Fe Literary Review

"There is no voice quite like his. What shines in every poem is musical sound and rhythm, grittiness, reality, humor, and the rare ability to tackle serious subjects without taking himself too seriously. There is a wonderful, refreshing lack of pretentiousness and self-pity in all his poems and books."
Alice Persons, Editor and Publisher, Moon Pie Press

"Morrison can be trusted to not waste your time; every poem is worth the read. It's a perfect book for late night with a drink…"
Paul 'Blowfish' Lovell, Boston Groupie News

"Dave Morrison loves his characters—their quirks and clutter, their errors and longings. He follows them into their houses, their laboratories, their two-bit convenience-store jobs. He watches a thief who hides "things/of value in the houses of/unsuspecting people." He ponders his namesake, King David, who "sinned mightily, but he wrote the psalms,/and had a bold heart, and I imagine he was doing the/best he knew how, as who he was." In "Black Crow," Morrison writes, "there must be something to justify/crow's obsessive curiosity." Crow's answer, and the poet's, lifts like a breeze from this buoyant collection: the urge to dream, to imagine, to stand "on the top of a tall mast in the sun . . . until the land [falls] away . . . obsidian star, carved coal angel, heaven above, earth below."
Dawn Potter - Author of Boy Land and Other Poems and Tracing Paradise

"A tidal wave of outrageous creativity; a wild rift of lines that leave you out of breath, fascinated, manipulated, articulated. Watch out!"
Elizabeth Garber, author of Pierced by the Seasons and Listening Inside the Dance

"By tapping into his tumultuous past, Morrison has created work that is not only technically sound, but viscerally engaging. His is no passive verse; it grabs you by the collar and demands your attention. "
Allen Adams, themaineedge.com

"So there's obviously no f**king with Dave Morrison's writing...read [it] by candlelight while drinking straight from the bottle, the radio playing softly in the corner."
Matt DiGangi, Editor Thieves Jargon

"These poems embrace a truth that includes success and screw-ups, love and loss, laughter and *life.* Poems such as "Fly" and "For the 9-Year-Old Victim" make us think about what preciously short lives we have, those like "Keith Moon" and "The Old Depression" lead to reflections on dreams and purpose and chances and self-destruction, while poems like "Marathon Man" and "My Jump Rope Song" and "Poetry Rocks" remind us how vital it is to laugh (and laugh at ourselves).
Donna Marie Merritt, Poet at AvalonPress, Author of What's Wrong with Ordinary?

"Morrison's rock star past haunts much of his writing, but his eye for detail and his razor-sharp sense of humor elevate his words into something much more than that — something visceral and anchored in the real world, whether it's in the past or the present."
Emily Burnham – Bangor Daily News

"Poem/portraits that are Rock-bottom genuine, totally direct, and disarmingly moving, packed with human attitude and artifact. He presents a cast of lonely figures filled with shy hope as they swing between the desire for the companionship of others and the frantic attempt to preserve their integrity."
Ted Bookey - author of Lostalgia

"There is very little academic about Dave Morrison's approach to poetry; he is a rule-breaker. Don't talk to him about sonnets or sentence structure. His poetry is uncontrived, and it is like breathing, sometimes long and steady; other times, choppy and quick about the lungs. But always, there is rhythm, and uncompromising honesty."
Lynda Clancy - PenBay Pilot

Stethoscope

Dave Morrison

JukeBooks

Grateful acknowledgements are due to the editors of the following publications where some of these poems first appeared:

The Maine
34th Parallel
Clare
Uni-Verse
Santa Fe Literary Review
Spillway
Dash Literary Journal

Library of
Congress Cataloging-in-Publication Data

Morrison, Dave

Stethoscope / Dave Morrison

ISBN 978-1-304-61537-4

For more information about Dave Morrison please visit
http://writerrocker.wix.com/davemorrisonpoetry
www.jukebookspublishing.weebly.com

As always, for Susan.

Still and all, why bother? Here's my answer. Many people need desperately to receive this message: I feel and think much as you do, care about many of the things you care about, although most people do not care about them. You are not alone.
Kurt Vonnegut

Contents

A Short Happy Life

When someone dies in their
prime, someone promising and
strong and beautiful we

are horrified that such a
thing could happen, we
question our god and

sneak peeks in the mirror,
we are shocked and disappointed
that they were denied the

chance to grow old.
Conversely, in heaven the
strong and young and

beautiful are congratulated
like lottery winners for
having a

short happy life.

Accident

The magic, the exhilaration is in
the shock of the transition: one
moment all the elements of your
small universe are in proper
order, and then in the time it takes
to cough, or snap your fingers or
say 'Jack Robinson', in that tick of
the second hand it's a whole new
world filled with almost unbearable
excitement and immediate peril -
the wheels and the road are no longer
speaking to each other, the language
of start/stop/left/right is no longer
in use, your body, like a well-trained
fireman has leapt into action by
tensing every muscle and
spraying the inside of your chest with
adrenaline. What was once a familiar
landscape of vertical trees and telephone
poles, a grid of asphalt streets, sensibly
placed houses; these have been replaced with
this excruciatingly beautiful wide ribbon
that wraps around your windows, every
color in the rainbow going sideways like
the twirling dress of a gypsy dancer, it's
an amusement ride come to riotous life,
this tops-eye view of your new world;
what was once a predictable automobile
is now a centrifuge, a roulette wheel, a
spinning coin, and in those hour-long
seconds you wonder what will bring
this ride to an end - pole, tree, truck,
stone, maybe a giant child's hand?
All you know is that it won't end well,
it can't end well, so you take the
practical approach; enjoy the ride,
whoop and wave your hat like a
bronc buster, look for the blurred
faces of your family and friends

while the calliope pipes its lusty
jubilant song and your wooden
stallion rises into the
neon-blasted night.

After Dark

She prayed for peace because
she was afraid that her heart
would fly apart from spinning
so fast,
because her thoughts were a
busy highway that she needed
to cross but couldn't.
Her hungers exhausted her,
her despair drained her;
where was the rest? Bursting
with enthusiasm, sodden
with ennui, falling in love
at the drop of a hat,
distracted

After she had given up
expecting it she realized
that she had grown into
peace, into the pleasant
rhythm of a pleasant life
not governed by want or
impulse but by a quiet
purpose and acceptance.

It was less rich than she'd
hoped. Less passionate. It
had no smell. She was grateful,
like when a hangover goes
away, but she found herself yearning
for a little chaos, for bright colors and
loud noises, for lust and sex and
disappointment, for whiskey and
music and strangers, for things that
happen after dark, for that sometimes
delicious uncertainty.

Assumptions

Let's assume that all is well.
Let's assume that every challenge or problem or surprise can be dealt with.
Let's assume that the Universe is on our side.
Let's assume that people are fundamentally good.
Let's assume that everything will work out in the end.
Let's assume that it's going to be a good day.
Let's assume that good intentions are important and will be honored.
Let's assume that people will disagree with us and that is fine.
Let's assume that the Past and the Future are not as important as Now.
Let's assume that our neighbors and coworkers are doing the best they can with what they have.
Let's assume that we are loved for all the right reasons.
Let's assume that we are forgiven, and so should forgive.
Let's assume that we are blessed and the blessings will keep coming.
Let's assume that none of us is any better or worse than our neighbor.
Let's assume that you can live any way you choose as long as you don't hurt anyone.
Let's assume that death is not anything to be afraid of.

Baby Jeesus
(for Lady J.)

The old fisherman was
repairing nets on
the beach. His neighbor
and her niece were
having lunch on
a rock.
He looked up from
his work with a
start and cried out
"Baby Jeesus! Where'd
you get to?" Clambering
to his feet he struck a
pose that he would assume
many times each day,
fist on hip holding his
weathered cap while
energetically scratching
his gray scalp.
She laughed and called
out "He's asleep in the sand
behind your boat, you old
fool!"
He knelt in the sand. Baby
Jeesus awoke and gazed
up at him lovingly.
"Don't you leave me now,"
the old man whispered,
"what would I do without you?"
He scooped up Baby Jeesus
and rubbed his head - Baby
Jeesus licked his nose.
He placed the precious bundle
on the beach, and it took off after
a seagull. She laughed at the tiny
legs that could move so fast.

"Will you look at that Baby Jeesus go!"
The girl asked why he would give his dog such a name.
"Ain't his dog." she said.

Backwards

I wake up an old
man, dizzy, stiff-jointed
and slow. I shuffle
downstairs to make
tea, barely ready
for the day.
By midday I'm at
my peak, a do-er.
By dusk I will be
a lazy teenager,
interested only in
drinks + smokes +
movies.
I will climb into
bed and become
a happy baby,
dreaming in a
salty sea.

Barely Stand It

Her name must be
Elaine - all her friends
are calling her Laney.
Long sun-honeyed hair
knotted at her neck, soft
cotton shirt, cut-off jeans,
flip flops, comically
over-sized sunglasses.
She is long-limbed and
summer-fresh, she throws back
her head and laughs and I
fall in love.
The young man with her shows
teenaged muscles, wears a
rawhide necklace, his hair is
tousled, his teeth straight and
white, and I fall in love with
him, too.
They pass an elderly man in a
bucket hat, newspaper and
cane and I fall in love again.
I fall in love with the delivery guy,
hand truck loaded with restaurant
supplies, I fall in love with the
lab on a leash, I fall in love with
my own pulse.
Maybe I fall in love too easily,
but the blessing of
growing older is learning that
what you thought were flaws
are often blessings.
It's like Groundhog Day with
my wife - every day, over and
over I fall in love.
Tonight I'll fall in love with a
glass of red wine, I'll fall in love
with our bed, and looking up through

the skylight I'll fall in love with
stars, blessings, mystery, darkness,
possibilities. Just before I turn out
the light I'll fall in love with my wife
again. When I close my eyes I'll fall
in love with God, and dreams.
So much love I can
barely stand it.

Binary

We live in a digital age;
0s and 1s
1s and 0s
two numbers, so
clean and simple and
efficient. In the old
analog days everything was
a complication of wires,
the multi-hued glow of
vacuum tubes, too many
choices, too much to
think about.
Now it's just
0s and 1s
yes or no
one thing or the other
black or white
right or left
blue or red
problem or solution
my way or the highway
with me or against me.
This is clearly a system
designed by modern
man.

Blind Test

Trust me, all we
care about is
competence. All that
matters is
quality. We may
hold the scales, but
we are blindfolded.

Some might say that
your gender dictates
whether or not you
are suitable - not us.
We don't take into
account your appearance;
we don't notice stylish
dress, a pleasing shape,
straight white teeth.
We could care less who
you love or have S-E-X
with.
Being a friend or
family member is
neither here nor there.
Your religious practices
are not our concern, neither
is your ethnicity, no matter
who you remind us of.

We are a blank white wall
that you are projected on.
We simply want someone
honest, hard-working,
reliable and capable, and
if that person happens to be
attractive and obedient and
malleable, if they do not

challenge us or cramp our
comfort zone, if they are,
in fact, just like us what
can we say?

These things happen.

Brahms, I Believe

There were six of us.
At first we tried to carry it
upside-down, the legs and
pedals in the air like a
stranded turtle's legs.
This only worked in
the open areas.

Then we tried removing
the legs and pedal lyre - four
lugging the piano itself,
two carrying the
amputated bits.

This allowed us to carry it
on its side which helped as
the trees grew closer, the
scrub and vines thicker.

We tried lashing it to
poles with the small amount
of rope we had, but no
matter what we tried it was
always slow and arduous work,
someone always walking backwards
or sideways, handholds slick with
sweat, drilled by mosquitoes.

Once while trying to lift it over
a fallen tree we dropped it -
what a horrible glorious racket
that sent every bird panicking
into the canopy.

Then we were five.
Then four, and those four
were skeletal and feverish and
spent. We found ourselves in

a clearing, the ground
uncharacteristically level and
solid.

Making use of what energy
we had left we carefully fitted
the legs and lyre back in
place and righted it.

Then, the one who
could play, did.

Bright White Stars

I've never seen a
night sky like
this one - it is a
child's sky, heavy
with blue/black crayon
and random daubs of
bright white stars,
stunning and beyond
words, like my love's
bare back or face
lit with laughter, or
a snowfall on a
rocky beach -
I salute these
failures of poetry
because as powerful as
words can be they
are often like us;
mute in the face
of indescribable
beauty.

Cannonball

Jump?
Fall?
All of a sudden it
doesn't matter.
This waterfall of wind in
my ears - this is where my
love of heights has gotten
me. I try to swim through
the air out of habit until
I am rescued by muscle
memory; it is Summer and
I am at the Town Pool,
hugging my legs into a
classic cannonball, a
dive meant only to get
attention and soak
onlookers, and it is
perfect, the roof of the
car conforming to my
shape while the glass
blows out in all directions
like a chlorinated tidal
wave and
I lie very still-
I lie very still-
paying attention to
everything, especially
the quiet.

Cigarettes

He was 20 years old,
playing in a band,
living in a drafty house
by the turnpike.

Most weeks he saved his change
for cigarettes, but this week
someone had given him a
coupon for a free carton of
a new brand.

At the Merit station on the corner
of Cambridge and Western the
clerk tried to force the carton
through the slot in the
bulletproof glass.

It would not fit and she would
not open the door, so she had
to pass the packs through the
slot one by one while
people waited to pay for
their gas.

Ten packs of cigarettes
in his pockets.
He had never felt so
rich and so
poor.

Coming To A Better Understanding By Contrasting One Thing With Another

The difference
between boredom
and a
glue trap
is that
the mouse
is terrified
and I
couldn't care
less.

Dark

I've been listening to
the dark for
hours.

At first it was
fine sand sifting
over old stones,

then warm wind through
a rusted screen,
then heavy mist

falling on the
roof of a
convertible.

The night was an
aquarium filled with
stones, each one a

worry, and the sound of
the darkness was
black ink poured in,

until there was nothing
but the sound of
the darkness, like the

hiss of a radiator in
the memory of
another house.

Dear Diary

On Monday everyone was fascinating on Tuesday everyone bored me to tears on Wednesday everyone was noble and/or wise on Thursday everyone was an idiot or worse on Friday everyone was dangerous, or at least undependable on Saturday I drank wine and everyone was my flawed but lovable brother or sister on Sunday I just wanted to be left alone on Monday everyone moved too fast on Tuesday everyone had forgotten about the $ they owed me on Wednesday everyone surprised me with their kindness on Thursday everyone got something that they didn't need on sale on Friday everyone let me down on Saturday everyone offered me a ride when my car wouldn't go on Sunday I vowed not to give a shit what everyone thought of me on Monday I wondered if I would ever learn to quiet my mind on Tuesday everyone broke my heart on Wednesday everyone repeated a lie on Thursday I was exhausted for no reason on Friday we all did something we thought we had to on Saturday I forgot and on Sunday I remembered.

Decision

The toddler falls on the
sidewalk and everything
stops; forward motion
has been interrupted by
some unseen obstacle
and now an assessment
must be made - there
is pain, there is
disappointment -
is it bearable? Can
it be faced alone or
is help needed?
The toddler experiments
with the faces that will
correspond to the reaction;
stoic, laughing, crying.
How best to deal with
this new situation?
Give in to the grief of
dashed plans, indignity,
the frustration of being
small and vulnerable?
And what about the pain,
why does that have to be
a part of everything?
The skin that was so soft
and perfect is a mess of
sand and blood, a miniature
model of how people can
be ruined.
But the toddler had been on
the way to somewhere to do
something interesting, and
not only is that possibility
still there, it's more urgent
than ever. There's so much
to notice (and isn't that what
led to the fall in the first place);
the color of the great tarp of

the sky, the invisible movement of the
air and the sounds and smells
it brings. There are people, colors,
even the gritty texture of the sidewalk
and the new fascination of the
scraped knee.
Wail or continue,
reach for big arms or
pull yourself up to your
wobbly feet, give up or
push on?
Think carefully baby, this
is a decision you'll make
every day.

Dressing Room Mirror at Macys

Trying on shirts.
Good god.
It looks as if I have deep-fried
and eaten the lithe muscular young
man I used to be, like I've been
sculpted from lard and I'm
standing in the sun.
My hair and head look like a
cheap doll that was left in
the woods. My teeth look like they
were carved and put in place by
someone with failing eyesight.
I vowed never to be like this.
There's no way my wife can
find me attractive. There's no way
any woman under 70 can find me
appealing, except as an organ donor.
I will never be hired again. I will never
write a good poem again. God will
deny having made me.
I only have two choices: change my life,
my diet, my exercise, my habits, or
stay away from mirrors.

Faith

Muslims believe that
angels are made of light and
record each person's acts.

Some Jews attach small boxes
filled with scripture to their
foreheads - others swing a
live chicken around their
head to transfer their sins
to the bird.

Christians believe that a man
built a massive wooden boat and
filled it with all the animals on
the earth to save them from the
flood that covered the whole
planet and killed everything
but the fish.

The Nation of Islam believes
that Allah was on earth in
the person of an Afghan
restaurant owner in Chicago.

Mormons believe that a man in
New York was guided by an angel to
gold plates buried in the ground that
were the source of the Book of
Mormon. The man translated them with
a seer stone that he put in his hat. The
plates disappeared before anyone else
saw them.

Scientologists believe that Xenu
brought billions of people to
earth 75 million years ago in
space ships.

So, assuming that it isn't that

difficult to get people to believe
wild tales and embrace outlandish
practices, here goes:

Last night the Great Goddess of the
Universe, creator of all gods and
creatures came to me in the form of
a huge beautiful eagle with an electric
guitar (a Gibson ES 335 dot neck of all
things with tone like you wouldn't
believe): and her eyes were fire that
did not burn and her voice was a
whisper that could be heard in all
eight corners of the globe, and the wind
from her wings was a hurricane of
pure love, and she said:

"Dave - be not afraid, but spread this
message to all the people and let them
know that these principles supercede
all others:
be kind
be fair
be honest
be sensible
be playful
be balanced
be curious
be forgiving
and above all keep a sense of humor and
don't take yourself too seriously. And if you
ever have to choose between love and
something else, choose love."

When I awoke these words were etched
in the fog of my bedroom windows as if
written with a feather -
I'm transcribing as fast as I can, but
they are disappearing in the
morning sun...

First Do No Harm

Just treat me the way
you would treat an
injured man waiting

for an ambulance: hold
my hand, stroke my
cheek, smile beatifically

and assure me that
everything is all
right, help is

on the way. Don't
give me details or
assess my condition,

I don't want to
know. I just need
medium-watt kindness

to distract me for
a few moments then
I'll be OK.

First Draft

The moon was massive and
orange and full, climbing slowly
above the treetops and into
the tattered black strips
of the clouds. It had the
faint hot menace of an unkempt
stray dog. The stars were
wild and the wind was like
fine sandpaper.
"Beautiful," she said, "it
looks too beautiful to be real..."

I'm sorry reader, I have to stop you
right there; this poem isn't really
going anywhere, it was just an
attempt to prime the pump, get
something going, to feel like
I'm doing...something. Yes,
moon, big, lovely, who gives
a shit? There's something
wordless and urgent that needs
to be illuminated and I can
only find it by patting around
the walls in a darkened room,
I have to fake my way in and
stumble blindly until my toe
hits something solid on the
floor, holy shit it's an unconscious
poem and it needs immediate
attention. Until I bring it back to
life I'm just one of those bored and
tired drivers holding up a name sign
at the airport:
Henderson?
Henderson?
Car Service?
They never showed but I picked up
a fare on my way back into the city
which is illegal but I can't have another
job where I pay more in gas than I make.

Home, late, tired I peel off my clothes
and drop them in a pile on the floor and
glance up through the skylight -
My god.
That moon, like
a massive pewter platter
hoisted into the sky, painting
the rooftops with this faintly
lavender half-light, its shine is
simply its loneliness for its
brighter love, burning on
the other side of the world.

For You

How can I tell you
that I believe in
you in a way that
gives you aid? Not
just comfort, or feeling
less alone, but in a
way that helps you bail
the water of doubt out
of your wave-tossed
boat?
How can I help you
believe that you will
get the relief that you
deserve even when
I don't know how or
when?
My love may not be enough.
There must be something I
can offer you to offset
what feels like
discouraging evidence.
Maybe it's just my
certainty that you are
doing the right thing,
and that is almost
always difficult. I
can't promise that
the payoff will be that
much sweeter, even if
I believe that that is so-
it's not about the payoff.
It's about faith and
effort and your true
heart, even when it
feels like a flickering
candle in a storm.
It is still light and warmth,
even if it is not what
you expected.

That only makes you
more brave.
That only makes me
believe in you more.

Gimmick

I looked in the mirror and
was disappointed:
not noteworthy
not noticeable
not memorable.

I thought about it
long and hard - not wanting
to be garish or tacky or
obvious, but tired of not
having a trademark, of being
invisible.

First I went to a haberdashery,
and tried on a derby, fedora,
pork pie, fez, beret, scully cap,
Cherokee headdress, and finally
chose a chrome welding helmet
with crow feathers and a rotating
light.

I bought a wooden vest and
aluminum spats, a leather bowtie
and silver bangles for my wrists.
An eye patch. Elbow-length
gloves. A working cuckoo clock
tie tack.

Satisfied with my choices I
threw then all out the window
on the drive home.

Next I went to a tattoo parlor where
I paid extra to have The Burning of
Joan of Arc tattooed on the inside
of my skin. I swallowed jewelry.
I braided my pubic hair, and got
contact lenses the color of my eyes.

When I walked into the crowded

room for my debut I got the response I wanted - a collective gasp at all that didn't show. I was strikingly unadorned, almost offensively normal, unnervingly plain. I had achieved the desired effect.

Good Soldier

As little boys we were
wired to fight; to pretend
to kill and die, to be heroic
and triumphant and merciless.

Now that I have little to prove
I'll tell you this - I would not
have made a good soldier, not
because I couldn't kill, but
because I'd be too scared to
stop.

He Only Meant to Borrow It

The night that Charlie took the truck
his father slapped him, spilled his drink
He sputtered "Boy, you pushed your luck,
the cops were here, you stupid fuck,
now what will all the neighbors think?"

His Mom had cleaned the kitchen twice
she looked for other things to do
she wished her husband could be nice,
but if she spoke up she'd pay the price
so she filled the salt, and pepper too.

The night that Charlie took the truck
he stuffed some clothes into his pack
"You don't much like me, do you Chuck?"
His father swung and Charlie ducked
and then he pushed his father back.

Hungry

Is a typewriter hungry for
paper? Hungry to be touched,
hungry for words? As a machine
perhaps 'hungry' isn't the proper
word, but it certainly needs those
things to live up to its purpose.
So, I'm not hungry in a literal
sense, but I do feel a yearning for
the exact same things for
the exact same reason.

I Want to Be That Guy

Very often a movie will
have a character, usually
a man, who lives quietly

among his neighbors in
a small tidy house with
a well-tended garden,

and for a while people
will whisper about his
past, doing something

dangerous or illegal or
interesting, but because
he is polite and keeps

to himself the talk about
his past will be replaced
with admiration for his

roses or the new color of
paint or how he helped that
young couple whose beater

broke down on the way to the
hospital, and even if on
occasion the light will strike

him a certain way or he'll get
a steely look in his eye that
gives you a little chill, for the

most part he'll just be one more
face at the town meeting, one
more middle-aged man at the

gas pumps thinking out loud
that it sure smells like the
snow is coming soon.

Luna

I go through
phases, like the
moon. I can be
so full that I
think I rival the
sun, plagiarizing her
light, claiming
the night sky as
my stage.
But I can also
be reduced to a
sliver, a fingernail
clipping, giving no
more light than a
cat's eye in a
distant headlight.
Full, empty.
Unmistakable,
invisible.
A mover of
tides, or a covered
mirror.
When full, anxious
of fading, when dark
jealous of light.
I sometimes think
I'd be better off as
a small steady star,
a pinprick exempt from
the pendulum of
change.
But then I'd never
light the way for
someone lost, or
give lovers an
excuse for an act
of daring.
I need to embrace the
changeability of
being. I need to be

grateful for my place
in the firmament.
I need to shine,
when I can.

My Essay

Is Poetry Dead?
While you're at it, consider
this; Is Tetherball Dead? How
about Paper Road Maps, or
Typewriter Repair? Is the
Yo-Yo Dead?
Isn't this *interesting*?

Is Poetry Relevant Today?
What about Neat Handwriting?
The Multiplication Tables? I
thought that ukuleles were dead
but now you can buy one at
Sears! Whatever happened
to Roebuck?
Isn't this *fascinating*?

No, I mean it, let's
Talk About Poetry. And
after that we can talk about
hiking, or cooking, or
swimming. You can go
to college to learn how to
talk about poetry - don't
you want to know what's
right, what's good? Thank
God, there are experts who
will tell us how to write, what
to write about, how to express
ourselves, how to be unique.

Interviews, essays, critiques;
never in the history of mankind
has there been so much talk about
poetry at our fingertips! Good
thing, because the best poems are
as indecipherable as the Bible in
Latin - how can we understand them
without help? You want to join a
secret society, forget the Masons -

become a poetry connoisseur.

Seriously folks, I'll give it to
you straight; poems will never
die - there's never been a
better or more democratic vehicle
for magic and stories and dreams,
and on a good day, truth; there's
never been a better way to get to
know ourselves, and each other,
there's never been a more pure
mode of creativity, there's never
been a better way to offer yourself
to the Universe. There will always be
poems, and people who write and
read them.

But back to the original question;
Is Poetry Dead?
My god, I hope so.

My People

My people gave us
Big Band music and Country
Western; we created the Masons
and the computer industry, we can
dance and cook and play hockey,
we are farmers and fishermen and
landscape painters and cowboys and
carpenters and bank executives.
We write historical non-fiction and
mysteries and yes, poetry. We built
highways and airports, we designed
cars, and wrote for TV.
We were once a vast proud people,
we were once dominant and important.

We'll be back.

My Waking Dream

from last night was that I
pushed up from the bed and
swam up through the ceiling

through the crawl space and roof,
pushing solid things aside as if
they were reeds, and somewhere

around 100 feet I broke through
and took a big delicious breath.
It was as if I were floating on the

surface of a deep crystal-clear
lake; I could look down and
see the tops of trees, roofs, roads;

I could surface-dive down and
look in the lit windows of
dark houses. Treading water I

wondered if I could swim up
through another layer of sky,
then another, and if I pushed

farther and farther through thinning
strata until I cross some kind of
border would I be like a fish that

propels itself up onto the sand?
Perish or evolve, ending or
beginning?

Mystery Man

He feels like some shadowy
figure has hired him to learn
everything about a
Mystery Man,
and that he is all three men.
He is an archaeologist exploring
his own tomb to try to imagine
what his life must have been
like, until he can't remember
who he is studying and
why it matters.
In moments of clarity he
sees what is coming; this
unimaginable state, this
infantile old stranger that
will bankrupt them and
turn his partner into a
tired full-time nurse.
He knows what he has to
do, he knows several ways to
do it, he will not leave a
mess for her in the giving
of this last gift.
The car, the shop-vac hose,
some duct tape, he can do it
in the wee hours and
play the radio low.
He is sharp, he is resolute,
this is the best he's felt in
months, he is his old self and
it breaks his heart.
The next morning he hears her
on the phone with their
son, worriedly relating how she
found him in the kitchen in
the middle of the night
clutching the car keys with
a faraway look. What was he
thinking?

Yes, he thinks, good question.
I wonder what I was
thinking?

One Difference

between the men and
the women in my family
is dirt; the men think of it
in terms of work, and the
women in terms of
shame.

Ordinary Day

Walking to work he
looks like any anonymous
middle-aged mid-level
drone: year-old chinos he
pressed himself, a polo
shirt of some color or
another, putting one foot
in front of the other, home
behind him, work ahead,
a day like a thousand others;
he is living clip art, he is a
demographic, he is of a
certain group.
He is undercover.
In the space between the
headphone earpieces he
is someone invisible to
the casual eye: he has a
secret, he has a hundred
secrets, he is a one-man
sleeper cell, he is achingly
alive, he is unbeatable, he
is quiet genius, and in this
case he is in the first row
of a Stones show at the
El Mocambo; he knows
the band, he knows the
songs, he can play each
instrument, he is watching
Little Sister dance, and if
he were walking on a dusty
road he would leave no
footprints.
He is in this world but
not of it, he is taking up
space but not really here,
he is exactly what he appears
to be and yet incomprehensible,

he is Adam trudging through
Time and he has just pecked
his way out of his shell to
witness, for the first time,
this astonishing, lovely,
ordinary day.

Pleasure Poem

This poem is not for
you, Professor -
not for you, Contest Judge,
Editor, syllable-counter,
grammar police, classics
disciple.

This poem is not for
you, boundary-pusher,
lover of the odd and
edgy.

This poem is not even for
you, dear friends.

This poem is for me.

This poem has no value
other than pleasure, like
skipping a stone or
singing in the car or
cooking a meal or
sculpting beach sand.

This poem is simply about
the satisfaction of creating
something where there was
nothing, about the pleasure of
watching the pen skate across
the empty page leaving its trail
of black string. This poem is a
little invention, a conjuring trick,
daubing color onto a fresh canvas.

This poem will not be published, maybe
not even read. This poem will not make me
the slightest bit rich or famous or
admired, but it will make me happy,
which is far more
useful.

Someone's Cranky…

In the old days we would
go down to the pub, the day's
work under our nails or ringing in

our ears; we'd be tired and slightly
pissed off and slightly joyous and
we'd bum cigarettes and order drinks

and we'd share news or tell lies or
start arguments or fall in love;
maybe we'd share some real grief or

fear or joy and maybe some truth or
comfort would come out.
Now what do we do?

Face Book, a dweeb computer
program invented by some Ivy
League kids; we sneak peeks at

work or we check in on our
little square phones.
Pathetic.

We have become an embarrassing
society. We've traded the pub for
goddam Face Book. And unless we

are in our own room we can't even
smoke. We'll die with a tumor behind
our ear and nice pink lungs, with

videos of cats dancing in our heads.
The Future is here, and if we call
now we can have a second one absolutely
free if we pay shipping and handling.

Special

Oh little baby you
are so special -
we know how Mary must
have felt, holding her
little world-changer.
You are smarter than
other babies, prettier.
You will make us proud,
you will bring honor to
the family, you will do all
the things that we didn't.

Oh young one, you're
falling behind, you've
got to keep up. You
were not born to do
OK, you were born to
lead, to be a star. You've
got to work harder, excel,
get the grades, the trophies,
the scholarships, fall in
love with a Winner.

Oh young adult, you had
such promise; you were the
brightest star in your class,
we had such plans for you.
Sure, you've got a good job and
a nice house and a place in the
community, but...
never mind. There's always the
next generation.

Oh, little baby you
are a miracle, you've
already won, you are so
perfectly you.

Stillwater

The siding salesmen came
through just as the pre-retirees
grew tired of painting the
once-grand Victorians
their parents left them.
To the practiced eye the
scar tissue of change is
visible along the river;
the rotted water wheel, the
blackened foundation of the
powder mill, the remains of
a dam, the pilings where the
shoe factory once stood over
the rushing water.

1000 mornings up at 4 am for
ice time, weights and Ben Gay,
the NY Rangers highlights videos
played over and over until they
snapped, the Pee Wee trophies,
the clippings from the local
paper, the partial scholarship,
the noncommittal scouts, move
back home. The over-sized
duffel jammed with pads and
skates rolls and thuds in the
trunk of his car like a body.

Driving to his job at Wal-Mart he
stops at the purposeless traffic
light downtown and watches the
flag snapping above the
courthouse.

It's like swinging from one rope
to another; how do you let go
of what was in order to grasp
what can be?

The Bather

I'm looking at a
painting by Cezanne and
trying to understand what

makes it 'good'. It is a
man in swimming trunks.
It is not accurate.

It is not beautiful. It
suggests that the artist
doesn't feel so good

about himself.
God damn.
I've just described

half of my poems.
I must remember
to wink.

The Count

My neighbor is a runner - every
evening in any weather, driven
by something I don't understand,
chasing something that I can't
see. He is lean and muscular and
oddly pale. His lights are on
late into the night - I've even
seen him puttering in his yard
in the dark, wearing a battery-
powered headlamp.
I suspect that he is a
vampire.

We love vampire stories because
no one wants to die. We don't even
want to grow old. The notion of
never aging is tantalizing, but
we know that it's unnatural, that
there must be some cautionary
element to the tale, so we learn
that vampires must drink blood.
Vampires must have this dirty
business that keeps them
going, driven by something that
we can't understand, lusting for
something we can't stomach, otherwise
we'd all want to be vampires and give
up on living good lives in hopes
of reaching heaven.

Older men admire younger women
for the same reason: they don't
want to die or grow old. Even if
it's just in their imaginations they
want to exist suspended in a time
when they are fresh and virile and
loaded with possibilities.

Instead, what if we aspired to being old and wise? What if we fantasized about being elderly and peaceful and preparing to die? What if we daydreamed about crossing the finish-line of a tiring and well-run race?

They're only words

they can't harm you;
on paper clusters of tiny bird
footprints, hieroglyphs, maps,
symbols, shapes drawn in the dirt
with a stick, traces of graphite, lines
of ink like the slick of a tiny black
snail, marks, scratches, stains.

To the ear they are just puffs of
breath chewed, kissed, bitten,
massaged; just a collection of
sounds put together like beads
on a string.

So why do I feel like words are
the bullets in a high-powered
rifle I have been given with no
training for its safe use? I just
want them to be small gifts,
morsels of food, the call of
a wise bird.

Thursday

I want to say something.
I want to say something
in such a way that hearing
it causes a swelling in
the chest.
I want to say something that
has the force of love behind
it like a strong wind blowing
open a door.
I want to say something
that nearly makes me
weep and makes me
question if I should say
it at all.
I want to say something
that peels away a veil
covering a mystery so
that the act of saying is
an act of discovery.
I want to say something
that is useful or comforting
or inspiring. I want to
perform that holy magic
trick where thought and breath
create art.
I want to say something
to clear the way for
another something to follow.

So today, for me, this
is poetry:
a space and the hunger to
fill it with something
good.

Vandal

At the hardware store I
buy gloves, a wire brush,
and lacquer-thinner, and
while checking out I
explain why and I want to
burn with righteous
indignation, but
I can't.

Graffiti.

Garish white paint
hieroglyphs on
hundred-year-old
brick.
Some kid, some
boy with no better
way to express himself;
he needs to exist, and
in order to exist you
first have to be
noticed.

I remember.

Maybe one day's worth
of anonymous notoriety
which on some days
is the best you can get, unless you
up the ante and do something
that will really get you
noticed.

Young girls rarely become
destroyers, classroom-shooters,
fire-starters - do they turn their
confusion inward, or are they

saving up their energy for
life-giving?

When I was young the more
daring among us would
climb the town water tower,
usually to announce our hunger
for powerful feelings by
painting a girl's name.

Maybe every community should
erect some tall dangerous
structure so our young people
can express themselves, and
feel a sense of risk
and accomplishment, and
exist.

Or, we could encourage the
writing of
poems.

Weather

Wall of fog,
sheets of rain;
this day has all the
components of an
old house - the
lightning a cracked
mirror, the sun a
dim bulb, the wind a
spirit moving from
room to room.

Wish

Listening to Beau Jocques while
I build salads, the slinky
zydeco makes me do my
happy awkward two-step
from the fridge
to the counter
and back.
I lose myself in the swampy
exuberance of it, but then
interrupt my own simple
joy by wishing that I could
play the accordion like that,
like a burly man blowing
beer breath through
ten harmonicas.

It happens all the time:
rather than simply enjoying
the gift of something
well done, I want to be
the one giving the gift;
telling the joke, hitting the
ball, dancing the merengue,
dropping from the high
dive like a hawk, building
something from scratch.

When I notice my wife
getting ready for bed and
wonder what it would be
like to be a beautiful woman
I know that I'd better sort
this out - why is everything
that I am not so enticing?
Why do I suppose that
some other version of my
life would supply some
missing ingredient?

I close my eyes, cross my fingers,
concentrate:

I wish that I were tall -
I wish that I could drive a stick shift -
I wish that I could play the guitar -
I wish that I had love in my life -
I wish that I could write poems.

I open my eyes -
all my wishes have come true.

Words

The teenager described some
everyday occurrence to his
friends, trying to fill the

empty hours of a fall evening
in a small town. It was important
that the tale suggest danger, or

recklessness, or the dark sheen of
adulthood, so the young man used
one of the few tools available;

language.

"Shit, man; bitch spilled the
whole motherfucking can right
down his motherfucking

keyboard. Damn." He glanced at
the girl to see if she was tuning in
to his edgy urban cable-comic vibe.

Growing up takes too long - a
young man has to accelerate things
with language, or cigarettes or

crime or drinking or sex or
something. Otherwise you can
be left behind, like a forgotten child.

"Un-be-fucking-leivable." He
spat on the sidewalk. "That
shit is ruined." He glanced at her

and she smiled. Another triumph
of motherfucking
language.

About the Author

High school graduate and above-average guitar player Dave Morrison was born outside of Boston in 1959, and played in rock & roll bands in Boston and NYC. He now lives on the coast of Maine with his wife Susan. Dave's poems have been published in literary magazines and anthologies and featured on Writer's Almanac and Take Heart. Stethoscope is DM's ninth book of poetry.

video still - Chris Lehmann

www.ingramcontent.com/pod-product-compliance
Ingram Content Group UK Ltd.
Pitfield, Milton Keynes, MK11 3LW, UK
UKHW041920190726
13854UKWH00003B/1356

9 781304 615374